KAMUI
カムイ
3
七海慎吾
Shingo Nanami

Other titles available from Broccoli Books

Galaxy Angel Beta

Commander Takuto Meyers and the Angel Troupe have evaded the evil Lord Eonia and successfully escorted Prince Shiva to the White Moon. But the danger is growing as the crew of the Elle Ciel and their newest recruit, Chitose, must prepare for their final battle. The Angel Troupe is about to face their greatest challenge in the conclusion to the Galaxy Angel series.

Story & Art by Kanan

Suggested Retail Price: $9.99 each

Volumes 1 & 2 available now!

Until the Full Moon

Marlo is half-vampire, half-werewolf with a problem. On nights when the full moon shines, Marlo undergoes a mysterious transformation... he turns into a girl.

Story & Art by Sanami Matoh

Suggested Retail Price: $9.99 each

Aquarian Age – Juvenile Orion

Sixteen-year-old Mana returns to her hometown and reunites with her childhood friend Kaname after 7 years. But he seems to have changed during their years apart. They soon discover that they are part of the Aquarian Age—a secret war raging for thousands of years—and Mana just might hold the key to end it!

Story & Art by Sakurako Gokurakuin

Suggested Retail Price: $9.99 each

Di Gi Charat Theater – Dejiko's Adventure

Dejiko has destroyed the Gamers retail store! Now it's up to her and the rest of the gang to search for the secret treasure that will save Gamers.

Story & Art by Yuki Kiriga

Suggested Retail Price: $9.99 each

Volumes 2-3 Coming Soon!

Di Gi Charat Theater – Leave it to Piyoko!

Follow the daily adventures of the Black Gema Gema Gang, as they continue on their road to evil.

Story & Art by Hina.

Suggested Retail Price: $9.99 each

Volume 2 Coming Soon!

For more information about Broccoli Books titles,
check out **bro-usa.com!**

KAMUI

BY SHINGO NANAMI

KAMUI Volume 3

English Adaptation Staff
Translation: Satsuki Yamashita
English Adaptation: Elizabeth Hanel
Touch-Up, & Lettering: Fawn "tails" Lau
Cover & Graphic Supervision: Chris McDougall

Editor: Dietrich Seto
Sales Manager: Ardith D. Santiago
Managing Editor: Shizuki Yamashita
Publisher: Kaname Tezuka

Email: editor@broccolibooks.com
Website: www.bro-usa.com

A BROCCOLI BOOKS Manga
Broccoli Books is a division of Broccoli International USA, Inc.
P.O. Box 66078 Los Angeles, CA 90066

First published in Japan in 2001 by SQUARE ENIX CO., LTD.
English translation rights arranged with SQUARE ENIX CO., LTD. and Broccoli International USA, Inc.

ISBN-13: 978-1-5974-1050-2
ISBN-10: 1-5974-1050-0

Published by Broccoli International USA, Inc.
First printing, February 2006

All illustrations by Shingo Nanami.

www.bro-usa.com

10 9 8 7 6 5 4 3 2 1
Printed in the United States

KAMUI

TABLE OF CONTENTS

CHARACTERS
カムイ

ATSUMA

A young man who is sent by his village in the north to retrieve the stolen sacred spirit, Okikurumi. He is infused with the spirit of an ancient sword.

KOJOMARU

The kamui of an ancient sword from Atsuma's village. In return for the use of his powers, Atsuma allows Kojomaru to fuse with his body. Despite his ability and age, he is both short-tempered and immature.

SUMIRE

NOA's second-in-command and Tensho (Commander of the Heaven Division). She is infused with the power of the wind.

SHUI

Second lieutenant of NOA who takes Atsuma under his wing. He is infused with the power of fire.

CHARACTERS カムイ

SHIKI
The top general of NOA. Despite assuming an air of royalty, he is unemotional.

AIKA
First lieutenant of NOA and Sumire's right-hand woman. She appears to be strict and uncaring, which comes from her reluctance to trust anyone but Sumire.

HYDE
Lieutenant general of NOA, he holds the number three position behind Sumire. As the Chisho, he is in charge of the Earth Division.

YANAGI
First lieutenant of NOA and Hyde's right-hand man. Although loyal to Hyde, he keeps in close contact with Shiki.

ANZU
Teenage cadet at NOA. She joins after her family dies in the earthquakes, but is actually scared of fighting and only wants to live a normal life.

TERMINOLOGY カムイ

Atanan - Monsters that suddenly appeared after the Grand Sinker.

Earth and Sky Division - The Earth Division is led by Chisho (Commander) Hyde, and the Sky Division is led by Tensho (Commander) Sumire. The Sky Division and the Earth Division are the two forces that form NOA's military strength. Although their names are Earth and Sky, this has no relation to their jurisdiction.

EDEN - A part of the former city of Tokyo that was protected from the earthquakes by the government research facility's barrier. It is now controlled by NOA.

Grand Sinker - The second of two great earthquakes that have left Japan devastated. The southernmost islands of Kyushu and Shikoku are both completely submerged, and a good percentage of the main island Honshu is left underwater.

KAMUI - A term used to refer to the spirits.

I'touren - A term referring to the spirit embodied by members of NOA. For example, Lady Sumire embodies the wind i'touren.

NOA - Stands for Noble Offensive Academy. It is a society of young men and women who have been infused with kamui in order to fight the atanan. It is backed by a government research facility that has been performing paranormal experiments on humans.

Okikurumi - An ancient spirit and the most sacred kamui that is stolen from Atsuma's village. Its disappearance has a key role in the recent natural disasters and appearance of the atanan.

Tohsu - A term used to refer to the powers used by members of NOA.

Chapter
10 the chosen path

IN ONE NIGHT, ONE MAN...
...DESTROYED AN ENTIRE WING ALONG WITH SEVERAL STUDENTS.
ARE YOU WASTING THE GOVERNMENT'S RESOURCES?

THAT'S WHAT THE ELDERS ARE SAYING.
HOW DO YOU PLAN TO DEAL WITH THIS, NOA GENERAL?

WELL, SHIKI?
RUSTLE

IT'S OBVIOUS.
I WILL DESTROY THE PARASITE INFESTING NOA.
THE ONE CALLED ATSUMA.

EVEN IF HIS WAVE IS LIKE YOURS.

YOU HAVE BEEN HOLDING NOA TOGETHER THROUGH SHEER FORCE OF WILL.
I GIVE YOU CREDIT FOR THAT.
BUT YOU ARE NOT TO TOUCH HIM.

YOU WILL OBEY WITHOUT QUESTION.
I GAVE YOU YOUR POWER,
SHIKI.

YOU DO WANT TO STAY WITH NOA, DON'T YOU?

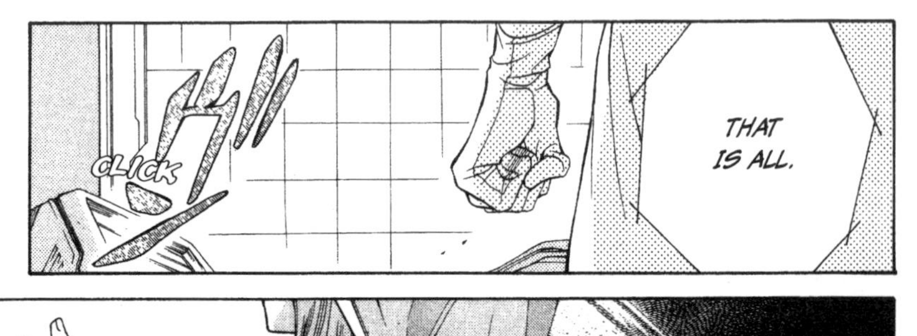
CLICK
THAT IS ALL.

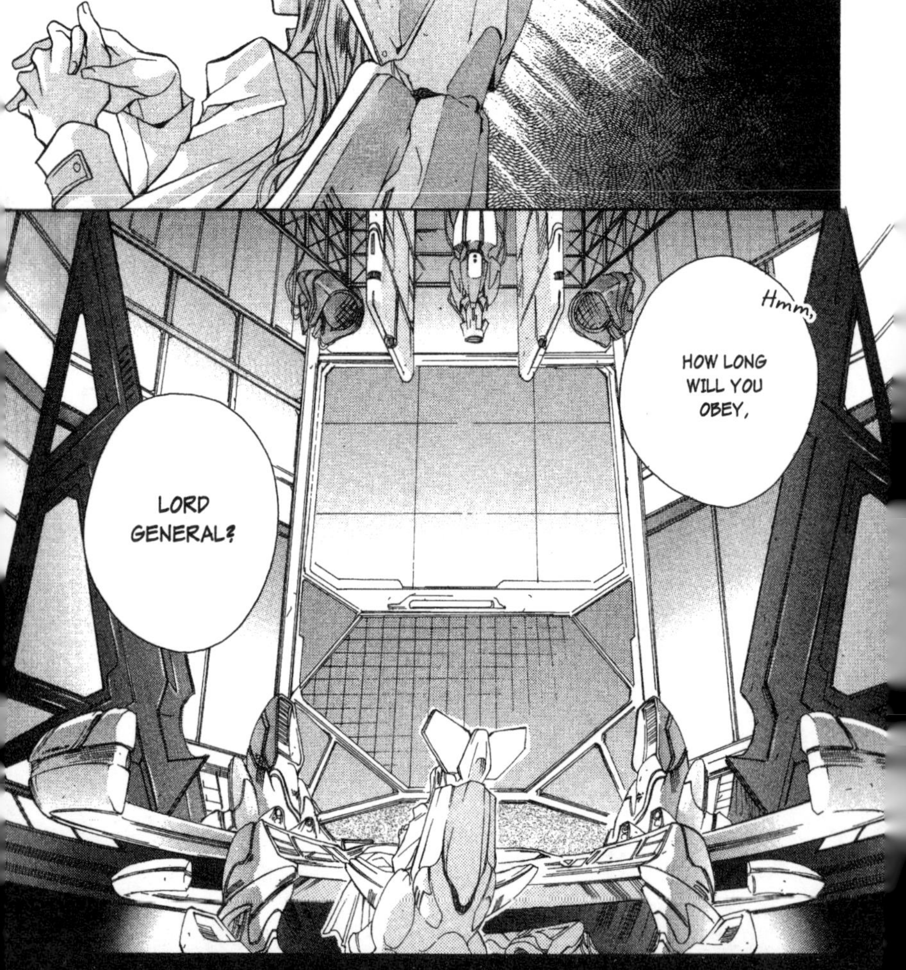
Hmm,
HOW LONG WILL YOU OBEY,
LORD GENERAL?

ANYWAY, AT THE END OF THE GAME...
...THE USELESS PIECES MUST BE SACRIFICED, EVEN THE "KING."
IT'S JUST...

...A MATTER...
...OF WHEN.

BLOOP
LORD HYDE.
I CAME TO SAY GOODBYE.
BUT YOU CAN'T HEAR ME, CAN YOU?
SCREEK
......!
YOU SEE, LORD HYDE.
I NEVER REALLY...
...BELONGED TO YOU.
BLOOP
BLOOP
BUT IT WAS FUN WHILE IT LASTED, WASN'T IT?

GOOD-BYE.
MY PRETEND MASTER.
RUMBLE

click
SO PRE-DICTABLE...
...RIGHT UP TO THE END.
Flip
ONE MORE TASK ON THE LIST.
Hmm
BUSY BUSY.
I DON'T HAVE TIME TO FEEL THE PAIN.
A NEW STAGE HAS BEEN SET.
BUT WHEN THE CURTAIN RISES...

...IS UP TO OUR NEW STAR.
YOU CLOSE YOURSELF OFF...

...SO YOU WON'T FEEL THE PAIN.
click

SHUI IS WORRIED ABOUT YOU, ATSUMA.
DON'T BOTHER ME.
IT DOESN'T CONCERN YOU.

MAYBE SO.

BUT I'M NOT GOING TO JUDGE YOU,
NO MATTER WHAT YOU DO.
OR WHAT YOU THINK.

EVEN IF CLOSING YOURSELF OFF...
...MAKES HER SUFFER.
OR...
...IS THAT WHAT YOU WILL SAY...
...TO HER?
"IT DOESN'T CONCERN YOU."
"YOU CAN BE HURT IF YOU WANT TO."

BUT YOU CAN'T SAY THAT.
YOU SAY YOU WANT TO BE ALONE.
BUT YOU'RE A LIAR.
YOU'RE LYING TO YOURSELF, AND THAT'S WHY IT HURTS.
ATSUMA.
IT'S NOT...
...A LIE.
CLENCH
I DESTROYED IT ALL!

THE HALL. THE STUDENTS. EVERY-THING!
I DON'T KNOW WHAT HAPPENED.
BUT I DIDN'T WANT THAT!
I DIDN'T WANT TO DESTROY EVERY-THING.
THIS PLACE SHE LOVED.
THIS PLACE THAT MADE HER SMILE.
I WAS FINALLY STARTING TO UNDERSTAND.
BUT I DESTROYED IT ALL!
AND I DON'T KNOW ANYTHING ANYMORE.
ATSUMA.

EVEN IF YOU DON'T UNDERSTAND, AS LONG AS YOU FELT SOMETHING,
THEN IT'S OKAY.
WHAT SHE WANTS FROM YOU...
...AREN'T WORDS,
BUT FEELINGS.

HAVE YOU REACHED OUT TO ANZU,
WHO MADE EVERY EFFORT TO REACH OUT TO YOU?
WHAT WAS SHE WISHING...
...FOR YOU?

I want to...

...watch you do that.
step
step
I...
step

!...
I NEED TO...
...MOVE ON FROM NOA.
BUT BEFORE THAT THERE'S A PLACE I NEED TO GO.

BEEP
BEEP
THERE IS SOMETHING...
...INSIDE ME, CONTROLLING ME.
WHEN THE GRAND SINKER STARTED THE DESTRUCTION...
...MY VILLAGE NEEDED TO DO SOME-THING.
IN ORDER TO PROTECT THEMSELVES,
THEY FORCED ME INTO A CONTRACT.

THEY INFUSED ME WITH THE KAMUI OF A SWORD CALLED KOJOMARU.
AND ORDERED ME TO USE ITS POWER TO STOP THE DESTRUCTION.
KOJOMARU TOOK MY BODY AS COMPEN-SATION...
...AND MADE A CONTRACT TO KEEP ME UNTIL THE RETURN OF OKIKURUMI.

SINCE THAT DAY, I HAVE HAD NO FREEDOM.
BUT IF I HADN'T LEFT THE VILLAGE,
I WOULD HAVE NEVER KNOWN...
...HOW MUCH IT HURTS TO CAUSE OTHERS PAIN.
OR HOW MUCH YOU CAN LEARN,
FROM OTHER PEOPLE'S WORDS.
I DIDN'T COME HERE IN SEARCH OF SOMEWHERE TO BELONG.
I DIDN'T COME LOOKING FOR FRIENDS.
I DON'T EVEN CARE ABOUT COMPLETING MY MISSION.

WHEN I CAME HERE,
I JUST WANTED TO BE FREE.

BUT NOW,

I WANT TO KNOW TRUE FREEDOM.

THAT'S WHY I MUST KEEP THE CONTRACT.
I WILL BREAK THE SHACKLES THAT HOLD ME.
I WILL RETURN TO MY FORMER SELF.

AND...
...FIND MY FREEDOM.
THAT'S THE PATH...
...YOU SHOWED ME.

Please walk the path you need to.

I want to watch you do that.

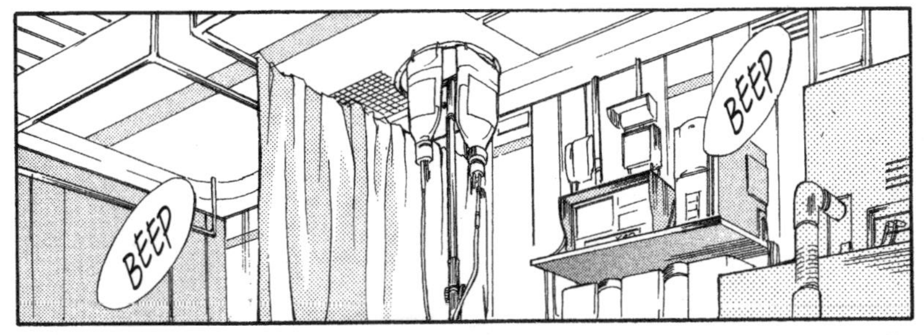

I'M SORRY.
THANK YOU,
ATSUMA-SAN.
BEEP

I THOUGHT...
... IF MIRACLES REALLY DO EXIST,
THEN I COULD JUST WAIT TO SEE HIM AGAIN.
BUT I'VE DECIDED NOT TO WAIT FOR A MIRACLE ANYMORE.
I WILL DESTROY NOA, THIS CAGE THAT HOLDS ME HERE.
AND GO TO THE RESEARCH FACILITY WHERE HE IS.

YOU SEEK FREEDOM.
AND I SEEK A BOND.
I WILL MAKE...
...A MIRACLE WITH MY OWN HANDS.
DO AS YOU WISH.
STEP
NOW THAT THAT'S SETTLED,
WOULD YOU...

...LIKE TO HIRE...
...A GUARD DOG?
SHUI.
I HAVE NO USE FOR GUARD DOGS WHO EAVESDROP.
OH KITTY.
PINCH
YOU'RE SO MUCH FRIENDLIER NOW!

CLINK
PLUS I HAVE...
...SOME QUESTIONS FOR THE KING TOO.

LIKE, WHAT HAPPENED TO MY SUPERIOR?
AIKA?
I HAVEN'T SEEN HER SINCE THE NIGHT OF THE PARTY.

SHE COULDN'T GO ANYWHERE IN THE STATE SHE WAS IN.
AND SHE WOULDN'T LEAVE YOU ALONE, LADY SUMIRE.
THERE AREN'T MANY PEOPLE WHO CAN DO ANYTHING TO HER.

SO I FIGURED I'D GO DIRECTLY TO SOMEONE WHO WOULD KNOW THE DETAILS.

YOU'RE WORRIED ABOUT AIKA?

WHEN THE SUPERVISOR IS AWAY, OUR DUTIES ARE DELAYED.
YOU CARE THAT MUCH ABOUT HER?

WHAT, ATSUMA?
ARE YOU...

...JEALOUS?
PINCH

DOES THIS MEAN I CAN COME ALONG?
Hm.
I GUESS SO.

RING
I CAN'T BELIEVE IT.

THAT YOU, ATSUMA...
...WOULD ALLY YOURSELF WITH OTHER HUMANS.
I WILL MAKE SURE YOU KEEP THIS CONTRACT.
WHOOSH

I WILL GET RID OF YOU.
Aha
I DON'T CARE.
Aha
AS LONG AS WE GET CLOSER TO OKIKURUMI.

WE MAY HAVE DIFFERENT REASONS FOR THE JOURNEY,
BUT OUR GOAL IS THE SAME PLACE.

THE TRUTH LIES...
RUMBLE
...WITH SHIKI...
...AND WHOEVER IS BEHIND HIM.

Chapter
11 fabricated reality

PLEASE STAY BACK, LADY SUMIRE!
THIS IS GENERAL SHIKI'S JURIS-DICTION.
YOU MAY BE THE TENSHO,
STEP
BUT WE CANNOT LET YOU THROU...
WOOSH

YOU DON'T UNDERSTAND, DO YOU?

SHIKI LEAVES YOU USELESS GUARDS HERE...
RUMBLE
...JUST TO POINT THE WAY.

IT'S NICE IN HIS OWN WARPED WAY.
HE KNEW WE WERE COMING,
AND PREPARED A WELCOME.

BUT HE WON'T BE PREPARED FOR US.
RIGHT, ATSUMA?
ZING
WHAT'S WRONG?

BA-DUM
DO YOU FEEL IT?
BA-DUM
YEAH.
THIS WAVE.
BA-DUM
IT'S THIS WAY.
BA-DUM
OKIKURUMI IS HERE?
I DON'T FEEL ANYTHING, THOUGH.
Huh?
IT'S IMPOSSIBLE FOR YOU.

OKIKURUMI IS ALWAYS SLEEPING.
How mean.
SLEEPING?
ITS WAVE IS TOO WEAK FOR YOU TO FEEL.

I'VE NEVER SEEN IT.
EVERY-THING IS TOLD IN STORIES.
BUT OKIKURUMI ONLY SHOWS ITSELF TO THE ONE WHO AWAKENS IT.

AND USING ITS MIRACULOUS POWER,
IT GRANTS THAT PERSON'S WISH.

IT GRANTS...
...YOUR WISH.
HAS ANYONE BEEN GRANTED A WISH?
IT'S FORBIDDEN TO APPROACH OKIKURUMI.
THOSE TEACHINGS...
...HAVE BEEN KEPT BY MY VILLAGE, ALONG WITH AN ANCIENT SONG.
A SONG?
SLEEPING CHILD, PURE AND INNOCENT.
EYES IN THE DARKNESS, WHO WILL GIVE IT LIGHT?
WHEN IT'S TIME TO WAKE, ALL WILL BE GIVEN.
NEITHER KAMUI NOR HUMAN,
IT IS A LIVING MIRACLE, CHILD OF LOVE.

NO ONE MAY TOUCH IT.
DOOM TO THOSE WHO BREAK THE COVENANT.
HEY,
HOW DO YOU KNOW THE SONG?
RUMBLE
THE GREAT EARTH WILL SHAKE,
AND WITHDRAW ITS PROTECTIVE HAND.

ROAR
BRINGING DESTRUCTION...

...TO ALL.

crackle

GO BACK TO YOUR DUTIES, SUMIRE.
roar
I CAME ALL THIS WAY TO SEE YOU.
YOU'RE SO COLD TO SEND ME AWAY.

YOU COULD AT LEAST ENTERTAIN US.
TAP
HOW MANY...
...TRICKS DO YOU HAVE UP YOUR SLEEVE?

SHIKI,
I'M GOING TO MAKE YOU...

...SHOW ME THE TRUTH.
HUFF
HUFF
HUFF
GASP
SLUMP

HUFF
SLIDE
WHERE AM I?
WHAT HAPPENED TO ME?
ARGH.
MY BODY... MY MIND.
IT FEELS LIKE I'M COMING APART.

AFTER I FELT THAT WAVE, I COULDN'T STAY IN CONTROL.
SOMETHING INSIDE ME...
...IS STIRRING.

AWAKENING FROM SLEEP.
IS IT RESPONDING TO THAT WAVE?
STOP IT.
DON'T...
DON'T CALL FOR ME.
I HAVE TO GET BACK.
OW
THE ONLY ONE.
I MUST RETURN TO HER.
LADY SU...

LADY SUMIRE!
SLAM

WHAM
ARGH!
WHAT DID YOU WANT ME TO SHOW YOU?
SCRUNCH
!
SUMIRE.
CHINK
SWISH

BAM
WHOOSH
THAT SWORD CAN CUT THROUGH AN ATANAN'S OUTER SHELL...
CLANG
KA
BOOM

Aha-
haha
SHOULD I TAKE OVER FOR YOU?
YOU CAN'T BEAT HIM BY YOURSELF, ATSUMA.
BAM
BAM
CRASH
BAM
NO WAY.
I'M NOT ASKING FOR HEL...
!!
WHOOSH
!
!?
VOOM

SIZZLE
EXCUSE ME.
WHY DON'T YOU TALK TO ME...
flutter
...A LITTLE?
WHAT ARE YOU DOING HERE,
SHUI?
LIKE I SAID...
GRAB

FLIP

CAN WE COOL DOWN A BIT...
VOOSH

...AND TALK CIVILLY?
KA
BOOM
WHAM
ROAR
MAYBE...
...YOU'LL SETTLE DOWN...
rub
ROAR

ARG!
SLAM
UGH!
THUD

WOOOO
KA
BOOM

WHOOSH
ROAR

SHIVER
SUMIRE.
CRACK

STOP THIS FUTILE RESISTANCE.
STAY BY MY SIDE AS THE HEAD OF NOA.
GRIP
DON'T YOU DARE ASPIRE FOR MORE AS LONG AS I AM HERE.
SLOP
THERE'S ONLY ONE THING I WANT.
twitch
WHIRR
twitch

HE DOESN'T WANT YOU.
YOU WERE LEFT BEHIND IN THE FABRICATED REALITY.
SO WHAT DO YOU WANT?
FABRICATED?
NOA
SWISH
THAT MAN TOOK YOU...
...AND DRAGGED YOU INTO NOA.
THE REAL PURPOSE IS...

...TO
DESTROY ALL
KAMUI.

!
THE GODS CALLED...
...ATANAN.

ATANAN ARE...
...GODS?
WHAT DO YOU MEAN?
MANY KAMUI GATHER, CREATE A FORM, AND BECOME A GOD.
ATANAN ARE THE MESSENGERS OF THE KAMUI THAT APPEAR WHEN MANKIND HAS SINNED.
THEY BRING ATONEMENT.

THE ATANAN ARE BRINGING ATONEMENT?
NO.
THE MADNESS OF THIS CITY IS MAKING THE ATANAN CRAZY.

I TOLD YOU.
EVERY-THING IS...
...FABRICATED.

THE GRAND SINKER THAT CAME SUDDENLY.
THE FEAR OF DESTRUCTION THAT SURROUNDS THE CITY, AND THE ATTACKS OF THE ATANAN.
TO SAVE THE WORLD, YOUTHS WITH POWER ARE ASSEMBLED IN AN ORGANIZATION.
THAT IS WHAT WE SEE.

BUT WE HUMANS ARE MISTAKEN.
THE RESEARCH FACILITY, IN SEEKING KNOWLEDGE, STEPPED INTO THE WORLD OF THE KAMUI.
IT STIRRED UP THE ANGER OF KAMUI, AND BROUGHT DOWN DISASTER AND DESTRUCTION ON THE CITY.
THE RESEARCH FACILITY BATTLED THE ATANAN WHO CAME FOR REVENGE.
AND SECRETLY USED EXPERIMENTS TO PRODUCE YOUTHS WITH THE POWER TO FIGHT AGAINST THEM.

THAT IS HOW NOA STARTED.
WE ARE MERELY PAWNS...
...OF THE RESEARCH FACILITY WHICH DESTROYED THE WORLD BY ANGERING...
...THE KAMUI.

SO WHAT DO YOU PAWNS...
...WANT FROM THAT MAN?
WHY?
CRUMBLE
HOW CAN YOU KNOW ALL OF THAT...
...AND STILL...
...DEFEND NOA?

I DON'T CARE...
...ABOUT THE TRUTH.
RDAR
SUMIRE.
IT'S BECAUSE I FOUND YOU.

001
SUMIRE.S
A SINGLE BUTTERFLY...
...HELD IN A CAGE CALLED NOA.

EMPTY EYES WITH NO FEELING.
CORDS AND WIRES DANGLING FROM HER THIN LIMBS.
UTSUHO?
A BEAUTIFUL BROKEN DOLL.
THAT CALLED...
...A SINGLE MAN'S NAME.

Chapter 12 beyond the visible

3 YEARS AGO
TECHNOLOGY GREW DAILY WITH NO CARE FOR THE CON-SEQUENCES.
EDEN WAS STILL CALLED TOKYO.
AND NO ONE KNEW THE GRAND SINKER WAS COMING.

WHEN I JOINED THE RESEARCH FACILITY EXPERIMENTING WITH HUMAN DEVELOP-MENT...
...YOU AND THAT MAN WERE ALREADY THERE.
SWISH

HOW IS SHE?
SWISH
THE AFTER EFFECTS OF THE EXPERIMENT AND THE SIDE EFFECTS OF THE DRUGS ARE STILL BEING MONITORED.
SHE'S CONFUSED, AND HAS NO SENSE OF SELF.
SHE THINKS ANYONE WEARING A LAB COAT IS YOU,

PROFESSOR HASUMI.
SQUEAK
YOU'RE WRONG TO SAY...
...ANYONE IN A LAB COAT.
LOOK.
>>>RECORDED
FOR ANYONE ELSE, SHE IS NOT ONLY UNRESPON-SIVE...
...BUT VIOLENT.
BUT SUMIRE CAN RECOGNIZE YOU.
IS THERE SOMETHING SPECIAL ABOUT YOU?

TO INFUSE HUMANS WITH THE STRANGE POWER KNOWN AS TOHSU,
THAT IS THE PRIME DIRECTIVE OF THE RESEARCH FACILITY.
BUT ONLY ONE SUBJECT MADE ANY PROGRESS.
SUMIRE SENOU.
THE MAN WHO BROUGHT SUMIRE WAS THE PROJECT DIRECTOR.
UTSUHO HASUMI.
WELL, YOU ARE THE SON OF DIRECTOR KENJOU.
MAYBE IT'S YOUR NATURAL CHARM.
smile
SHIKI.
....
THE SUBJECT WHO HAD NO SENSE OF SELF...
...CALLED JUST ONE PERSON'S NAME.
BEEP
THE TEST

BEEP
WARNING ON THE VITAL SIGNS MONITOR.
BEEP
THERE'S AN ABNORMALITY IN THE PULSE AND BRAIN WAVE.
PRO-FESSOR HASUMI,
IT'S DANGEROUS TO CONTINUE THE EXPERI-MENT.
WE CANNOT AFFORD TO LOSE THIS VALUABLE SAMPLE. WE MUST STOP.
CAN YOU HEAR ME,
SUMIRE?

STAND UP AND CONTINUE.
WE'RE NOT DONE COLLECTING THE DATA.
PROFESSOR HASUMI?
twitch
SHE'S ALREADY BEEN PUSHED BEYOND HER PHYSICAL LIMIT.
SHE CAN'T GET UP.
I DIDN'T CARE...
GRIP
...WHAT STRONG BONDS...
...HELD THEM TOGETHER.

number/001
SUMIRE SENOU
STEP
STEP
FOOLISH GIRL.
I'VE SEEN PLENTY OF EXPERIMENT SUBJECTS.

MOST DIE FROM THE PAIN AND MISERY.
HUMANS WITH NO FAMILY, TOSSED OUT OF SOCIETY.
EVEN THOSE SCUM TRY TO ESCAPE FROM THEIR CAGES.

BUT SHE DIDN'T EVEN CRY.
SHE JUST HELD THAT MAN IN HER GAZE.
BUT WHY?
Mmm...

UTSUHO?

UTSUHO.
RRRRRR...

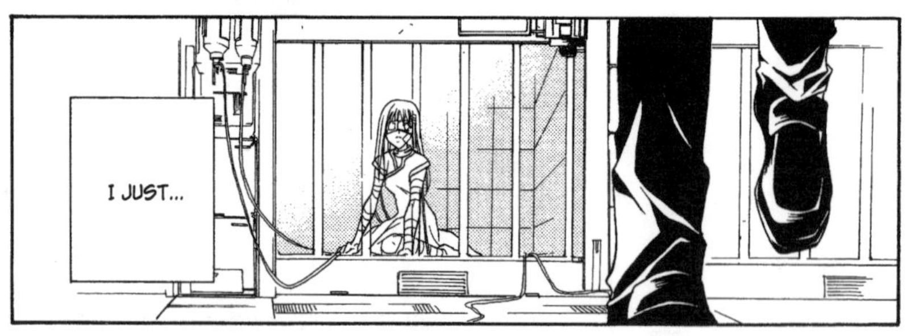
I JUST...

...WANTED TO GET HER OUT...

...OF MY SIGHT

step
step
BLOOD?
THAT'S...
...PROFESSOR HASUMI'S AREA.

RUMBLE

BLOOP
!!
SHOOOM
WHAT'S THIS!?

EVEN IF YOU ARE THE HEIR OF THE RESEARCH FACILITY...
...YOU SHOULDN'T ENTER RESTRICTED AREAS.

YOU'RE NOT THE FIRST INTRUDER.
I REALLY NEED TO IMPROVE SECURITY.
PRO-FESSOR HASUMI!
WHAT'S GOING ON IN HERE?
step
ALL THESE...
...SHAPELESS SUBJECTS!?
step
BLOOP
WHAT ARE YOU...
...AND THE RESEARCH FACILITY...

...TRYING TO DO HERE!?
step
I DON'T HAVE ENOUGH.

I NEED...
...MORE.
PAWNS.
!?
SHIKI.
WHAT ARE YOU TALKING ABOUT!?
THIS COUNTRY IS SOON GOING TO BE SWALLOWED BY AN EARTH-QUAKE.
A HUGE NATURAL DISASTER TO BE CALLED THE GRAND SINKER.

KYUUSHU AND SHIKOKU WILL SINK FIRST.
THE COUNTRY WILL CRUMBLE, AND A WORLD OF RUIN AND MADNESS WILL COME.
THOSE WHO SURVIVE WILL SEEK SALVATION IN THE MIDST OF DESPAIR.
THIS RESEARCH FACILITY AND YOUTHS WITH SUPERNATURAL POWERS WILL SAVE THEM FROM THE EARTH-QUAKE.
AND THEY WILL GLADLY SUBMIT TO OUR NEW RULE.
IN THESE HAPPY TIMES, IT'S HARD TO FIND THE NECESSARY SUBJECTS FOR THE EXPERIMENT.
BUT ONCE THE WORLD IS BROKEN, HUMANS WILL DO ANYTHING TO SURVIVE.
AND SUBJECTS WILL COME FLYING INTO MY HANDS.

OH,
SO MANY, IT WILL ALMOST BE FUNNY.
click
WHAT...
...ARE YOU...
...PLANNING?
FLUTTER

STEP
WHAT CAN YOU DO,
EVEN IF YOU KNOW?
ALL THE SUBJECTS,
THE STAFF OF THE RESEARCH FACILITY,
THE PEOPLE OF THIS COUNTRY,
SUMIRE,
YOU,
tap
THE KAMUI,
THE ENTIRE WORLD...

...ARE ALL MY PAWNS.
RATTLE
RATTLE
...HO?
UTSUHO.
NO.
UTSUHO.
NO!
RRRR
UTSUHO.
DON'T YOU GET IT!?

HE WON'T COME NO MATTER HOW MUCH YOU CALL HIM.
IT'S NOT JUST YOU. HE SEES NO ONE.
NOT EVEN THE WORLD.
YOU DON'T EVEN KNOW WHO YOU ARE. YOU'RE DISGRACE-FUL.
IS HIS NAME THAT IMPORTANT!?
OF COURSE.

I NEVER HAD MYSELF TO BEGIN WITH.
I KNOW MY NAME BECAUSE HE CALLS ME.
I KNOW MY BODY BECAUSE HE TOUCHES ME.
WHAT...
...ARE YOU SO AFRAID OF, THAT YOU CLING TO ME?

WHAT!?
YOU CLING TO ME WITH FRIGHTENED EYES.
clang
AREN'T YOU...
...THE ONE...
...CLINGING TO ME?

BY PRETENDING YOU KNOW NOTHING.
WHAT DO YOU WANT ME TO DO?
DON'T YOU REALLY WANT TO ESCAPE?
OR DO YOU JUST WANT MY PITY AND KINDNESS?
Hmf
WHAT CAN...
...YOU DO?
YOU CAN'T BREAK MY CAGE AND SET ME FREE.
OR EVEN TOUCH ME.
GRAB

BAM
!?
CREAK
SUMIRE
GENOU
WHY?
WAS THIS CAGE...
...ALWAYS OPEN?
Hmf
WHAT CAN YOU DO?
Hmf

YOU HAVE NO POWER.
YOU CAN'T HOLD ME LIKE HE DOES.
AND LIKE THIS CAGE...
...YOU AREN'T THE ONE WHO KEEPS ME HERE.
THAT...

...WAS THE ONLY CONVERSATION I HAD WITH HER THEN.
HER MIND WAS SOON CONFUSED AGAIN.
WAS SHE ONLY PRETENDING?
DID SHE ONLY COME TO HERSELF THAT ONE TIME?
IT DIDN'T MATTER.
SUMIRE WAS BEYOND MY UNDERSTANDING.
A STRONG AND NOBLE WILL,
SUMIRE
FILLED WITH LONELINESS.
AND THAT WAS WHEN...
...I REALIZED THAT MY ANGER TOWARDS SUMIRE...
...WAS JEALOUSY.
MY FEAR OF HIM, THE FEAR OF THE FORESEEN FUTURE.
IT ALL DISAPPEARED.

ONLY MADNESS ...
SHIKI KENJYOU
...WAS LEFT.
SHIKI AGREED TO HELP WITH THE EXPERIMENT.
IT'S ALL BECAUSE OF YOU.
HE WILL DEFINITELY BE OF GOOD USE TO ME.
YOU'RE A GOOD GIRL, SUMIRE.
THIS BUTTERFLY IS YOUR REWARD.
THERE YOU GO.

SHIKI.
YOU'LL RECEIVE THE POWER OF THE KAMUI.
BY HAVING TOHSU LIKE THE KAMUI,
YOU WILL HAVE THE POWER TO DESTROY THE KAMUI.
THAT DAY WILL COME SOON.
AND ONE MORE THING.
IF YOU SURVIVE...
...I WILL PREPARE A REWARD FOR YOU TOO.

A CAGE CALLED NOA FOR A BUTTERFLY.
I KNOW THAT YOU WILL...
...TAKE VERY...
...GOOD CARE OF IT.
WHEN I RE-COVERED,
AND I WAS ABLE TO WALK AROUND,
YOU APPEARED IN FRONT OF ME...
...FUNCTIONING PERFECTLY.
001 SUMIRE.9

YOU LOST YOUR MEMORY...
...OF WHEN YOU WERE CONFUSED.
EXCEPT ONE THING.
UTSUHO.

002
SHIKI.K
WHAT I TRULY GAINED...
STEP
...WAS NOT TOHSU OR THE RANK OF GENERAL.
BUT THE POWER TO KEEP YOU CONTAINED,
STEP
AND NEVER LET HIM TOUCH YOU AGAIN.
STEP

YOU WANT ME TO WITHER...
Whoosh
...IN A CAGE THAT YOU GUARD?
I HAVE NO DESIRE TO FULFILL YOUR NEEDS.
EVEN IF YOU WERE TO WITHER.

ALL I WANT...
...IS FOR YOU TO REMAIN IN MY HANDS.

GRIP
YOU...
...AND HER.
NOA AND THE WORLD.
AND MYSELF.
WE ARE ALL...
...BEING USED BY HIM!
UTSUHO!
IT'S TRUE THAT ALL HE SAID CAME TO PASS.
NO MATTER WHAT HE IS DOING OR WHY,
I WILL CONTINUE TO DEFEND NOA.

IF YOU WANT TO DEFEND IT, DO SO.
I DON'T WANT TO DESTROY NOA.
BUT I CAN'T STOP HERE.
I HAVE MY OWN PURPOSE.
THUMP
SWOOSH
STEP
THIS WAS ALL A TRAP?

SHUI.
YOU CAN HELP THE RESEARCH FACILITY...
...BUT WE WILL DO WHAT WE HAVE TO.
NO MATTER WHAT YOU SAY, I JOINED NOA FREELY.
THERE'S NO TURNING BACK NOW.
SO...
...WE'LL GO AFTER WHAT WE WANT.
IF NOT AT NOA, THEN AT THE RESEARCH FACILITY.
ATSUMA WILL FIND HIS FREEDOM.
AND FOR ME...
...IT'S MY SUPERIOR.

I'M LIKE YOU, RIGHT?
I FOLLOWED HER INTO NOA BUT SHE FORGOT ABOUT ME.
BUT I WON'T GIVE UP.
WE HAVE...
...NO REASON TO STOP YOU.
BUT THAT MEANS...

...YOU HAVE NO REASON TO STOP US EITHER.

Chapter
13 transfiguration

THERE'S ONLY ONE...
...THING I WANT.
THERE'S ONLY ONE THING...

...THAT I WANT, TOO.
ROAR
WHOOSH
THAT'S WHY I SAID WE SHOULD TALK...
...BUT HIS ROYAL HIGHNESS WOULDN'T LISTEN. THIS WOUND IS KILLING ME.
ATSUMA, ARE YOU OKAY?
IT'S A LONG ROAD, AND YOU'RE ALREADY BEAT UP.

OH.
I GET IT.
DO YOU NOT WANT TO HEAR THIS VOICE?
gasp
WHAT?
THE PERSON WHO LEFT YOU, STOLE OKIKURUMI AND DISAPPEARED.
THE PERSON CONTROLLING THE KING AND NOA.
AND THE PERSON LADY SUMIRE CAN'T FORGET.
DON'T YOU GET WHY LADY SUMIRE KEEPS ME AROUND?
IS...
...ONE PERSON WITH THIS VOICE, RIGHT?

BONK
I DIDN'T MEAN TO HURT YOU.
THE PERSON I WISH WOULD REMEMBER ME DOESN'T AT ALL.
Oh well.

WHAT IS YOUR...
...RELATION TO HER?
You're like...
...A WIFE ASKING ABOUT AN OLD FLAME
ATSUMA.
GRRRR

SHE'S A CHILDHOOD FRIEND.
WE'RE TWO YEARS APART...
...SO SHE PROBABLY THOUGHT OF ME AS A BIG BROTHER.
touch
ANYWAY, SHE WAS ALWAYS BY MY SIDE.

SHE WAS STUBBORN AND CAREFREE.
ALWAYS ON THE MOVE.
AND I WATCHED OVER HER.

WHEN THE GRAND SINKER HAPPENED THREE SUMMERS AGO...
...THE LIVELY STREETS AND ALL OUR HANG-OUTS...
...CRUMBLED INTO RUINS.

AND BEFORE THE DUST WAS EVEN SETTLED...
...THE NOA RECRUITERS CAME.

I DIDN'T CARE EITHER WAY...
...BUT SHE REFUSED...
...WITHOUT HESITATION.
SHE WAS ALWAYS VERY MORAL.
AND OF COURSE SHE WOULD BE AGAINST SOMETHING LIKE HUMAN MODIFICATION.
BUT...

...EVEN THOUGH SHE WAS TRYING TO BE STRONG...
...HER HANDS WERE SHAKING.
I WASN'T WORRIED.
I ALREADY HAD EVERYTHING I CARED ABOUT.
I DIDN'T NEED ANYTHING ELSE.
BECAUSE SHE CHOSE TO STAY BY MY SIDE INSTEAD OF RUNNING FROM THE CHAOS.

...I FELT THAT NO MATTER WHAT HAPPENED...
...WE COULD LIVE TOGETHER FOREVER.
THEN HOW DID YOU END UP AT NOA?
SAME AS THIS TIME.
ONE DAY, SHE DISAPPEARED.
AFTER MONTHS OF SEARCHING...
...I FINALLY SAW HER.

NOT THE CHILDHOOD FRIEND I GREW UP WITH,
BUT A SUPERIOR OFFICER OF NOA.
......
THAT'S WHY...
...I'M SCARED THAT SHE MIGHT TURN INTO SOMEONE DIFFERENT AGAIN.
HER WAVE.
I NOTICED IT EARLIER.
BUT EVEN SO...
...I DOUBT SHE'LL CHANGE BACK TO HER OLD SELF.

SHE PROBABLY WON'T...
...REMEMBER YOU AT ALL.
THERE'S NOTHING I CAN DO ABOUT THAT.
I WENT FROM A CHILDHOOD FRIEND TO A SUBORDI-NATE.
BUT...
...I'M STILL IN HER WORLD.
THAT'S ALL I NEED.

YOU'RE...
...KINDA LIKE HER, I GUESS.

YOU'RE BOTH 16, STRONG-WILLED, AND DON'T PLAY WELL WITH OTHERS.
BUT YOU'RE NOT HER.
AND EVEN IF MY VOICE IS SIMILAR...
...I'M NOT UTSUHO,
ATSUMA.

I WON'T LEAVE YOU BEHIND.
!!
WHACK
OOF!
SO DON'T WORRY!
YOU LOOKED...
...LIKE YOU WANTED ME TO SAY THAT.

DON'T BE SO FULL OF YOURSELF.
I didn't ask you along.
throb
OH?
YOU STILL DON'T TRUST ME?
I KIND OF WISH...

!
...YOU WERE...
...MY BROTHER.
WHAT?
WHAT DID YOU SAY?
NOTHING.
?
CREAK
BY THE WAY...
...THIS LOOKS LIKE A RESERVOIR.
DO YOU REALLY FEEL OKIKURUMI'S WAVE FROM...

!
AIKA!?
WHY...
...ARE YOU HERE?

WHAT SORT OF STRICT SUPERVISOR PLAYS HOOKY?
YOU DIDN'T HAVE TO COME OUT HERE.
I CAN SHOW YOU WHERE TO...

WHO ARE YOU?

......
AIKA?
LADY SUMIRE...
...WHERE?
WHAT'S THAT?
GRAB
LADY...
WHAT'S WRONG WITH YOU?
WHERE?
WHERE?
YOU DISAPPEAR...
...WITHOUT A WORD.
AGAIN...
Ha.

RRRRR
DON'T TOUCH ME!
N...
NO...
NO!

No!
AR...

NO!
NOOOOO!
ATSUMA.
THIS LADY'S BEHAVIORAL PATTERN...
HER ABNORMAL SENSE OF LOYALTY AFTER THE EXPERIMENT.
THIS IS LIKE...
...THE IMPRINTING THAT OKIKURUMI HAS TOWARDS THE FIRST PERSON IT SEES.
WHACK
YEAH.
BUT WHY...

...SUCH A CHANGE?
I'M SCARED...
...KO...
...JO...
...MARU.
!?
MAYBE YOU PULLED THE TRIGGER,
ATSUMA-KUN.

WHAT ARE YOU...
WHEN YOU LET YOUR WAVE GO OUT OF CONTROL, IT CAUSED OKIKURUMI TO ACTIVATE.
AND A SUDDEN BURNING FLARED UP INSIDE OF HER.
SHE WAS STRONGLY AFFECTED BY OKIKURUMI, SO THE CHANGE SHOWED UP DIRECTLY.
I COLLECTED HER AND KEPT HER IN A CAGE TO FEED THE GOD.
AND TO STUDY HER.
IT SURPRISED ME WHEN SHE STARTED ACTING LIKE A CHILD WHEN SHE WOKE UP.
WITH NO ATTACHMENT TO LIFE, HER MIND WAS SWALLOWED UP EASILY.

WHAT A WEAK, BORING HUMAN.
WHAT'D YOU SAY?
clench
I GUESS SHE WAS COHERENT ENOUGH TO ESCAPE AND SEEK HELP.
BUT WHO WOULD WANT TO HELP HER?
YOU DON'T WANT TO DEAL WITH THIS, DO YOU, ATSUMA-KUN?
IT'S OKAY, ATSUMA.

I THOUGHT...

...YOU WERE SMARTER THAN THAT, SHUI-KUN.
YOU HAVE BAD TASTE.
YOU DON'T WANT TO DEAL WITH SOMETHING THAT CAN'T EVEN HOLD A CONVERSATION, DO YOU?

OR DO YOU JUST WANT TO TAKE HER DESPITE HER WISHES.
FOR YOUR OWN NEEDS?
WHAT A GOOD IDEA.
BUT I THOUGHT YOU WERE SMARTER TOO.
CLAP
YANAGI-CHAN.

I COULDN'T EVER...
GRAB
...BE HAPPY DOING THAT.

IT MEANS NOTHING IF IT ISN'T WHAT SHE WANTS.
I WANT HER TO BE FREE TO CHOOSE.
THAT'S HOW I'VE ALWAYS LIVED.

THEN YOUR DUTIES ARE OVER, RIGHT? SHE HAS NO SENSE OF SELF.
BUT SHE WANTS...
...TO GO BACK TO LADY SUMIRE.

......!

ARE YOU BROKEN TOO?
WHAT DOES THAT EVEN MEAN?
WHO KNOWS?

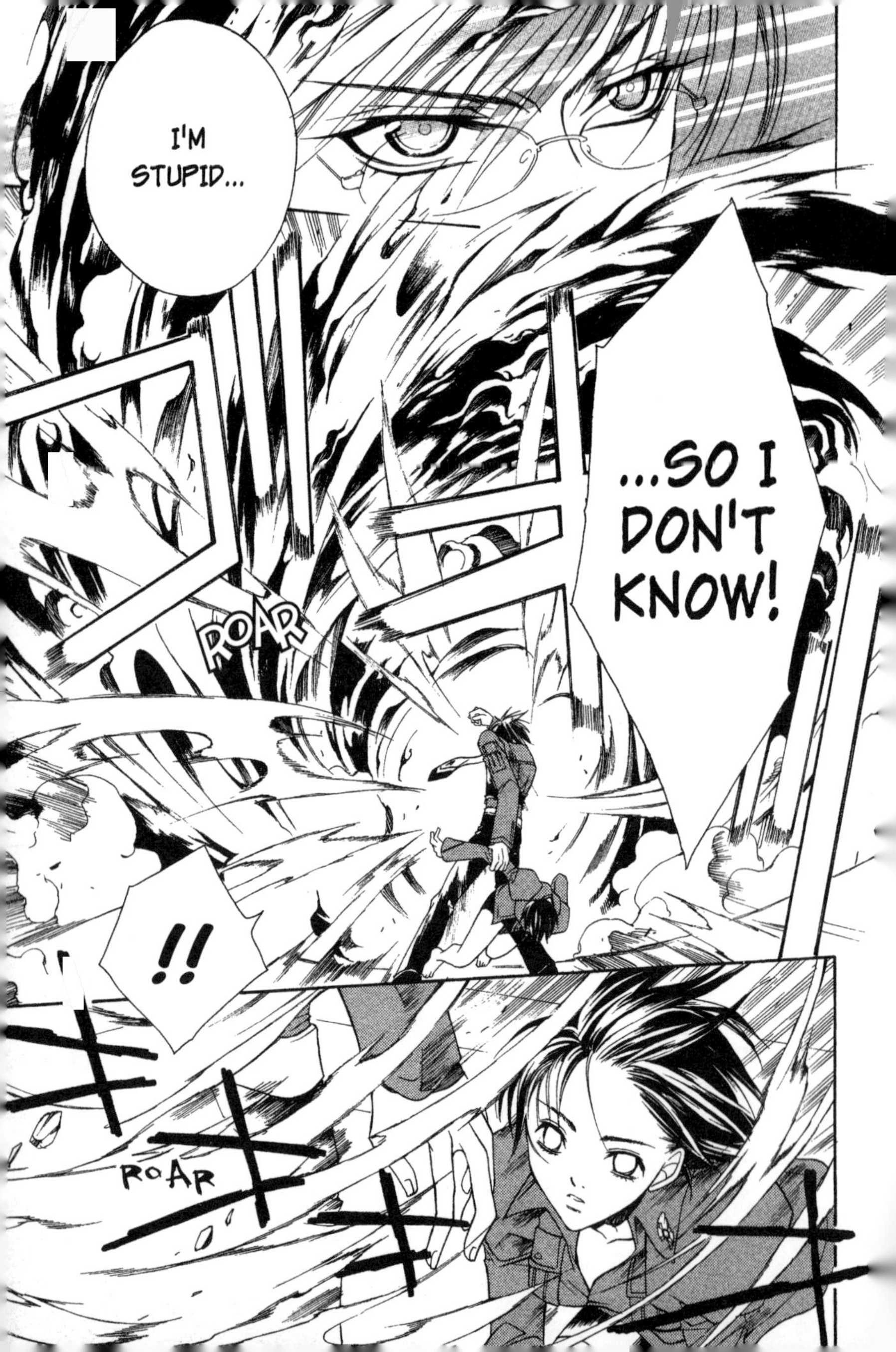
I'M STUPID...
...SO I DON'T KNOW!
ROAR
!!
ROAR

ROAR
ZING

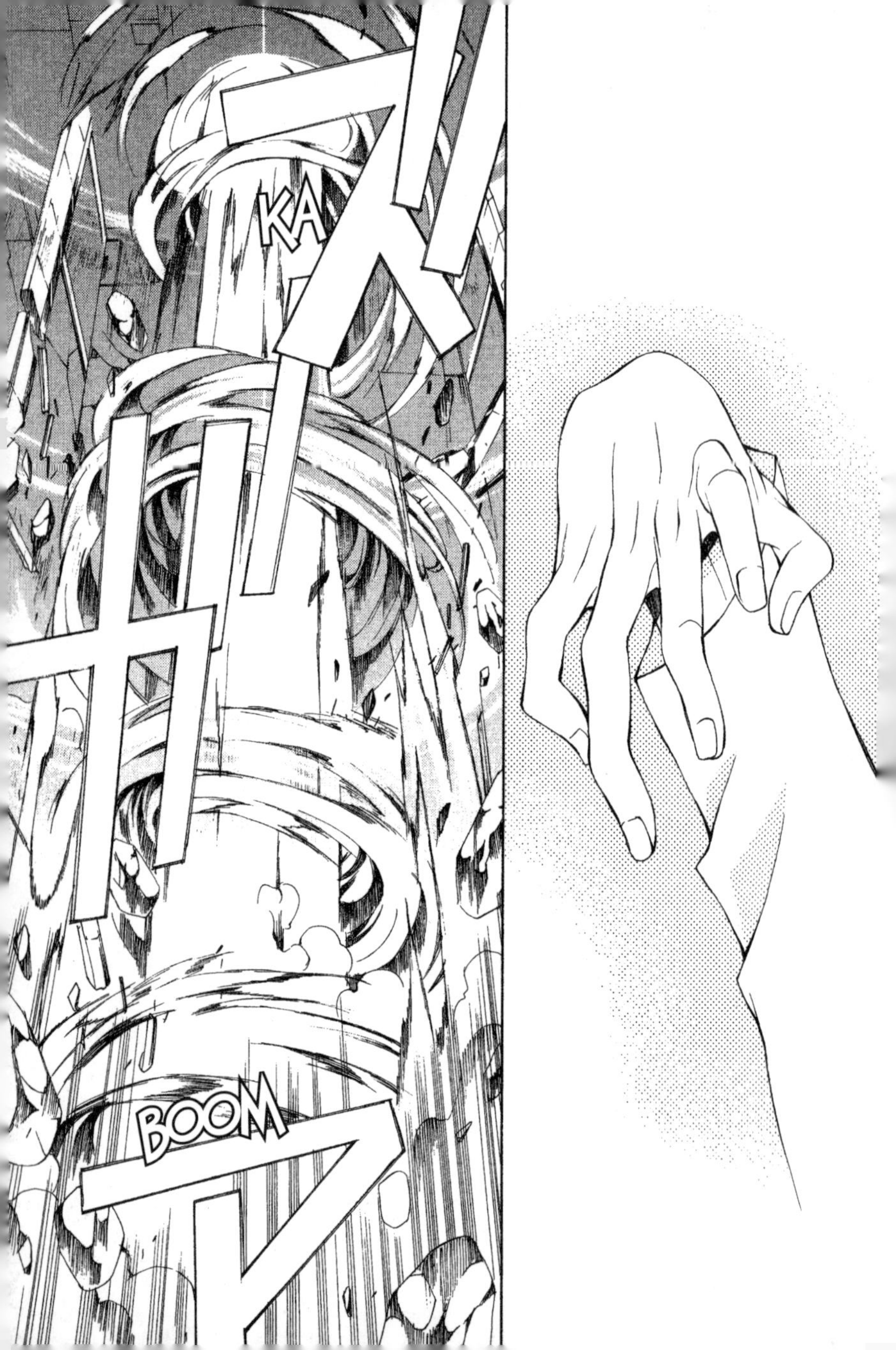
KA
BOOM

WHAM
......!?
THUD
IT'S NICE TO HAVE FUN CONVERSATIONS WITH YOUR FRIENDS.

THIS...
BUT YOU HAVE TO REMEMBER...
...THAT YOU'RE THE ONLY NORMAL HUMAN HERE AT NOA.
YOU SHOULD BE CAREFUL NOT TO HURT YOURSELF,
YANAGI.
MY APOLOGIES,
Whirr
...VOICE.

DON'T TOUCH ME!
Slap
YOU WERE FORCED TO MAKE A PACT WITH A KAMUI.
Hm
I GUESS YOU'RE STILL BEING ABUSED BY THE VILLAGE.
SHUT UP!
RRRR
I CAME HERE TO FULFILL THE CONTRACT,
...AND TO FREE MYSELF.
TO TAKE OKIKURUMI BACK FROM YOU...
IF YOU'RE GOING TO GET IN MY WAY...
I WON'T STOP YOU.
IT WOULD BE USELESS.

prince of our disorder
One more word
Chapter
14 my wish...

SMILE
UTSUHO!

PROFESSOR HASUMI.

USELESS?
THE KAMUI INSIDE OF YOU HELPED THE AWAKENING.
OKIKURUMI HAS ALREADY LEFT MY HAND.
ONCE IT STARTS MOVING...
ZING
...NO ONE CAN STOP IT...
ZING
...UNTIL IT AWAKENS.
YOU UNDERSTAND, SO BE A GOOD BOY AND GO HOME,
ATSUMA.
FLUTTER

OKIKURUMI...
...ISN'T YOURS!
OH, IT'S MINE.
BUT YOU SHOULD GO TOO,
I'LL THANK YOU FOR BEING USEFUL.

KOJOMARU.
SHUT UP!
BOOM
glare
GRIP
I WON'T GIVE UP.
IT'S ATSUMA'S FAULT.
IF YOU LEFT EVERYTHING TO ME FROM THE BEGINNING...
...I WOULD HAVE DESTROYED NOA, THE RESEARCH FACILITY AND ALL OF EDEN...
ROAR
...TO FIND OKIKURUMI.

LOOK, ATSUMA.
UTSUHO IS NOTHING TO ME.
ROAR
THAT'S WHY I HATE HUMANS.
THEY'RE WEAK, BUT THEY'RE SELFISH AND GREEDY.
I WON'T LET THEM...
...USE OKIKURUMI.
CRACKLE

FLOAT
!!
whoosh
WHAT!?
BUZZ
THIS POWER...
GRAB
I NEED TO PUNISH...
...KIDS WHO MISBEHAVE.
IF I TRY TO PUSH BACK...
...ATSUMA'S BODY...

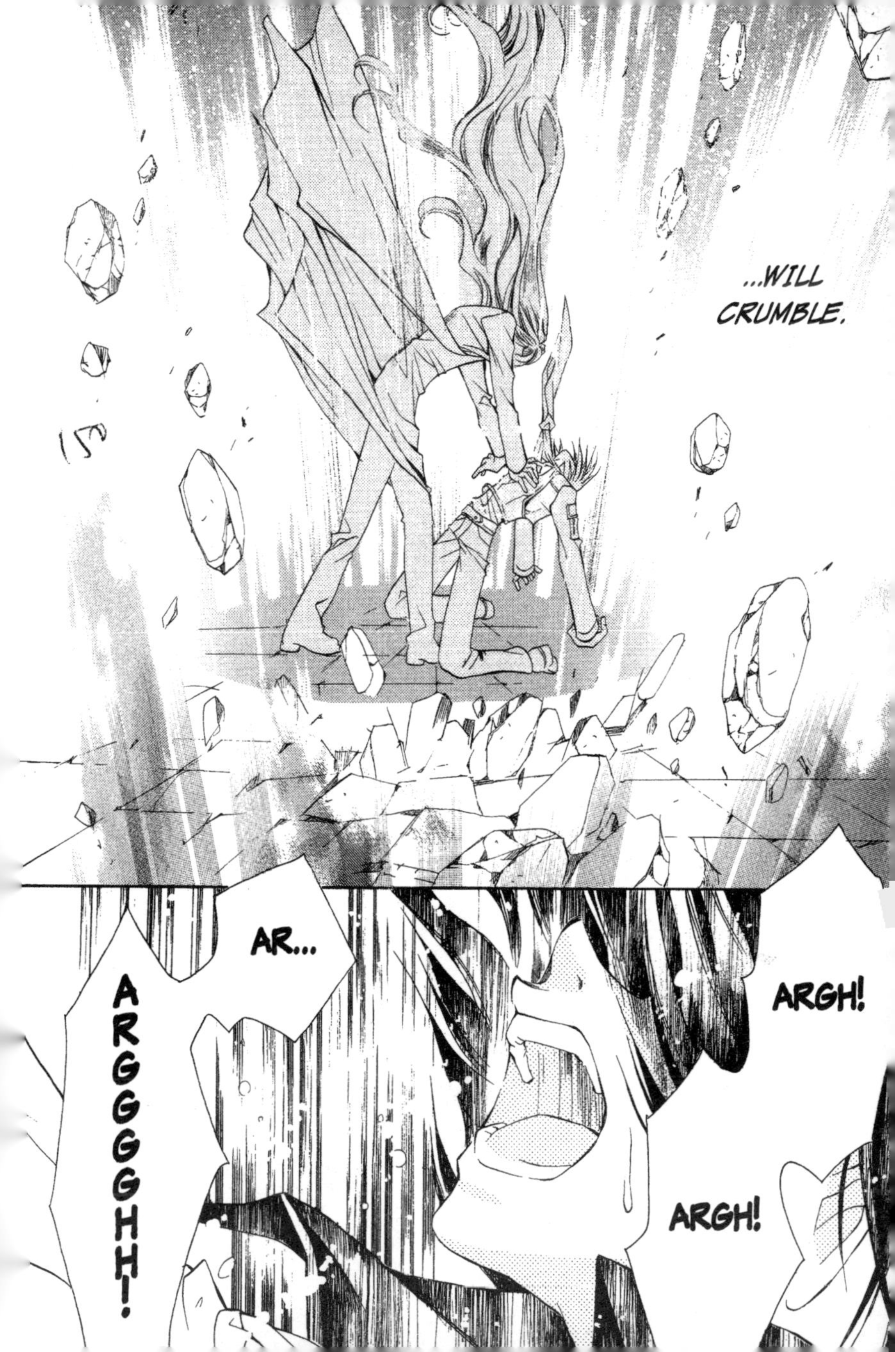
...WILL CRUMBLE.
AR...
ARGGGGHH!
ARGH!
ARGH!

ARGH!
AR...
AR...
AR...
AR...
ARGH!
ARG...
FALL
ARE YOU SATISFIED?

ATSUMA?
ZWISH
YOU HAVE NOW ACHIEVED YOUR GOAL.

GO WHEREVER YOU LIKE.
THUD
I DON'T HAVE TIME...
...TO PLAY WITH YOU.
SWAY
step

thump
touch
VOI...
Whirr
...CE.

CALL...
...MY...
...NAME.
drip
CALL...
TWITCH
AIKA.

CALL...
AIKA.
COME.
AI...
...KA?
RATTLE
OW.
WAS IT A DREAM?

GOOD GIRL.
WHAT DO YOU...
...PLAN TO DO WITH HER?
DON'T YOU KNOW, ATSUMA-KUN?

WE IMPLANT A CELL FROM OKIKURUMI IN A HUMAN BODY.
AFTER VARIOUS SYMPTOMS AND REJECTIONS...
...THOSE FEW WHO SURVIVE BECOME NOA.

THEY ARE REBORN WITH A BY-PRODUCT CALLED TOHSU.
THEY ARE THE ONLY ONES WITH A TRUE PURPOSE.
TRUE PURPOSE?

NOA IS AN ORGANIZA-TION TO MAKE HUMANS WITH TOHSU AND TO KILL ATANAN...
THAT IS TRUE. BUT WHAT WE REALLY NEED...
...IS NOT THEIR POWER,
BUT THEIR BODIES.
ALL ORGANISMS NEED NUTRIENTS TO GROW.
OKIKURUMI IS CURRENTLY TRYING TO GROW IN ORDER TO AWAKEN.

ALL THIS IS A TOOL PREPARED FOR JUST THIS MOMENT.
EDEN IS THE VESSEL IN WHICH TO GROW OKIKURUMI.
NOA SUPPLIED THE PAWNS TO PROTECT OKIKURUMI FROM ATANAN.
AND THE FOOD TO HELP NUTURE IT.
TO RETURN THE CHILD THAT WAS BORN FROM OKIKURUMI BACK TO THE WOMB.
WOOOSH
THAT WILL BECOME THE FOOD FOR OKIKURUMI.

AMONG THEM, THIS GIRL IS THE BEST.
THE MORE SIMILAR THE WAVE, THE BETTER THE NUTRIENT.
LOOK.
HUNGRY OKIKURUMI IS WAITING UNDER THIS WATERFALL.
drag
AIK...!

roar
DON'T FEEL BAD.
SHE CAME TO ME ALL ON HER OWN.
OH...
WHAT WILL YOU DO NOW?
...THE VOICE.
THERE'S ONLY ONE THING TO DO.

ATSUMA.
gasp

I...
I SAID DON'T WORRY, RIGHT?
TURN
I WON'T LEAVE YOU.
YOU MIGHT NOT BELIEVE ME...

...BUT REMEMBER.
I GOTTA GO FOR A WHILE.

TAP
clench

HE CHOSE HIS OWN PATH.
HE AND EVERYONE ELSE AT NOA...
...ARE ALL LIVING AS THEY WISH.
AND YOU AND I, TOO, OF COURSE.
YOUR WISH TO BE FREE CAME TRUE, RIGHT?
SO WHY...
...DO YOU MAKE A FACE LIKE THAT?
ATSUMA?

DON'T SAY MY NAME WITH THAT VOICE.
IF YOU HADN'T TAKEN OKIKURUMI,
I WOULDN'T HAVE SACRIFICED MY BODY TO MAKE A CONTRACT WITH KOJOMARU.
I WOULDN'T HAVE WANTED FREEDOM.

YOU TOOK IT AWAY FROM ME.
AN ORDINARY LIFE. ORDINARY RELATIONSHIPS.
MY FEELINGS AND EVERYTHING!

EVEN WITH NOTHING LEFT...
...BUT FEELINGS I HAD YET TO UNDER-STAND.
BEFORE I COULD CLAIM THEM, YOU DESTROYED EVERYTHING!
YOUR SHADOW ALWAYS HAUNTS ME!
I'LL NEVER FIND MY OWN PATH.

YOU TIED ME DOWN.
AS LONG AS YOU EXIST...
GRAB
UTSUHO!

...THERE'S NO REAL FREEDOM...
ROOAR
...OR RELEASE!

DRIP DRIP
WH...
WHY?
THUD

I DON'T CARE ABOUT THE REAL PURPOSE OF NOA.
I JUST HAVE...
...ONE WISH.

I JUST WANT...
...TO BE BY HIS SIDE.
Volume 03 END

This is the third volume. I still can't get used to getting older, but my body definitely gave up. I went to the doctor for hip pains. So sad.

But I've been able to keep going because of the support of my readers, editorial staff, and friends. Thank you very much.

At this time, I will include the character profiles that have been requested in fan letters. But I don't do a lot of set-up, so there isn't a lot of information.

Please continue to support them and the story.

I made it by hand.

← Eraser stamp

Shui
18 years old 180cm
Blood type O
He can do a lot of different things like cook and drive a car. He likes to take care of others. Likes silver accessories (like his chain and bracelet). He likes to sing. Probably very good at karaoke.
Cooking Recipe
Atsuma
16 years old
167cm
Blood type ?
This traveler from far away grew up in an isolated environment, so he doesn't know much about modern culture. He has probably never played a video game. He doesn't eat much. Light-weight.
intro-vert.
Aika
16 years old
155cm
Blood type A
Studious, serious and square. But she's a klutz. She likes sweets. Left-handed.
Thinking about why she failed.
Sumire
18 years old
163cm
Blood type B
She may look like a frail socialite, but she came from an average family, so she's pretty healthy. But she has no home-making skills. In some ways, she is unable to live on her own.

In this profession, letters are an important source of energy.

I would like to hear your opinions, so please write to me freely.

I'll see you in volume 4

BROCCOLI BOOKS
PO Box 66078
Los Angeles CA 90066
Attn: Shingo Nanami

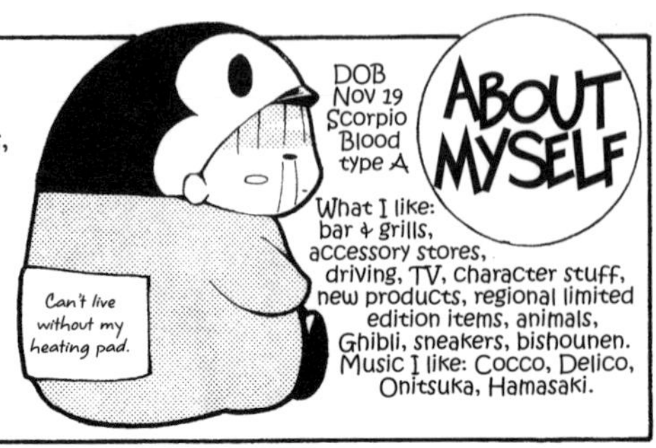

ABOUT MYSELF
DOB Nov 19 Scorpio Blood type A
What I like: bar & grills, accessory stores, driving, TV, character stuff, new products, regional limited edition items, animals, Ghibli, sneakers, bishounen.
Music I like: Cocco, Delico, Onitsuka, Hamasaki.
Can't live without my heating pad.

Kojomaru
Age ? 140cm Blood type ?
Carefree. Child-like Kamui.
Shiki
188cm Blood type A
He comes from a wealthy family. He grew up properly, so he doesn't like fussiness. His age is... well, he's young.
Yanagi
172cm Blood type AB
17 years old
A scientific genius. And he's very good at climbing the ladder. He is near-sighted with an astigmatism. He plays with his computer too much.
Utsuho
175cm
26 years old
Blood type ?
Everything is still a mystery.
Hyde
185cm Blood type B
He only takes care of things he likes. He does whatever he wants to others. Simple-minded. Direct and a bully. His age is... younger than Shiki.

TRANSLATION NOTES

カムイ

Pg. 33
San - A suffix; can be put after any name indicating respect.

Pg. 92
Kyuushu, Shikoku - Respectively, these are the second and fourth largest islands of Japan. Kyuushu is the most southerly, with Shikoku just to the northeast.

Pg. 133
Kun - A suffix, usually goes after a boy's name.

Pg. 137
Chan - A suffix; can be put after any name. It is often used for children, good friends or those younger than oneself.

Pg. 182
karaoke - A form of entertainment system providing prerecorded accompaniment to popular songs that a performer sings live, usually by following the words on a video screen. It is derived from the words "kara" and "oke," translated as "empty orchestra."

Ghibli - Studio Ghibli is responsible for such films as Nausicaa of the Valley of the Wind, Grave of the Fireflies, and the Academy Award winner Spirited Away. It is headed by world-renowned director Hayao Miyazaki.

bishounen - Literally "beautiful young boy," it is a Japanese word for "pretty boys." In the U.S., fangirls often refer to them as "bishies" for short. It can also refer to a style or genre of manga and anime which features bishounen.

Cocco, Delico, Onitsuka, Hamasaki - Cocco, Love Psychadelico (Delico), Chihiro Onitsuka, and Ayumi Hamasaki are all Japanese pop artists.

KAMUI

Utsuho's plan comes to fruition as Okikurumi begins to grow, swallowing up all living things around it. The spirit Kojomaru, now separate from Atsuma, finds his host broken and beaten in the ruins of NOA. With Utsuho's plan building momentum, there seems to be no hope. But the past comes to light and Utsuho's connection with Atsuma is finally revealed.

I'VE BEEN MEANING TO ASK YOU THIS FOR QUITE SOME TIME, YANAGI...
WHY IS MY HEAD CUT OFF IN THIS PANEL?
DON'T WORRY SIR. YOUR WHOLE FACE IS IN PLENTY OF PANELS IN THE NEXT VOLUME.

THIS PLACE WILL COLLAPSE SOON.
WE SHOULD HURRY...
Wheeze
WAIT...
DROP
...UTSUHO!
DROP

Wheeze
WHY?
WHY ARE...
...YOU DOING THIS?
Wheeze
OKIKURUMI.
ATSUMA.

RUMBLE
YOU AND I ARE NO LONGER CONNECTED.
YOU GOT YOUR FREEDOM. DON'T BOTHER ME ANYMORE.
I'M NOT...
...FREE.
IF YOU STILL THINK YOU'RE ATTACHED TO ME,
IT'S BECAUSE YOU ARE WEAK.
THUMP

WHAT?
YOUR WEAK MIND LISTENED TO THE VILLAGE ELDERS AND KOJOMARU,
AND YOU BELIEVED THE LIES THEY TOLD YOU ABOUT ME.
POINT
Swish
YOU BOTH ARE...
...ATTACHED TO A SHADOW THAT DOESN'T EXIST.

I HAVE...
...NOTHING MORE TO SAY.

GET OUT OF MY SIGHT.
WHY?
WHAT...
Wheeze
...DO YOU WANT TO DO?
UTSUHO?
ANSWER ME!

CLENCH
ANSWER ME...
...BROTHER!

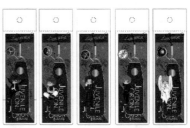

READ. POINT. CLICK.

www.bro-usa.com

After reading some Broccoli Books manga, why not look for more on the web? Check out the latest news, upcoming releases, character profiles, synopses, manga previews, production blog and fan art!

Galaxy Angel
BETA

Why settle for just one?
Galaxy Angel™
PARTY
Fifteen stories featuring the five lovely Angels!
With stories by Kanan, Botan Hanayashiki, Hina., Kazuki Shu, and more!
brought to you by
BROCCOLI BOOKS
www.bro-usa.com
© 2006 BROCCOLI
Illust. by Kanan.

Get Ready for Adventure!
ONLY DEJIKO AND HER FRIENDS CAN SAVE THE GAMERS STORE!
DI GI CHARAT THEATER
Dejiko's Adventure
TM
by Yuki Kiriga
brought to you by
BROCCOLI BOOKS
www.bro-usa.com

DI GI CHARAT™
The Original Series
© BROCCOLI • TBS
© 2005 BROCCOLI Illust. by Koge-Donbo
Synch-Point
AVAILABLE NOW ON DVD!
For more information:
www.bro-usa.com

EVIL HAS NEVER BEEN SO CUTE!
Leave it to Piyoko!™
B
© 2003-2005 BROCCOLI
Synch-Point
For more information:
www.bro-usa.com
VOLUME 1 AVAILABLE NOW ON DVD!

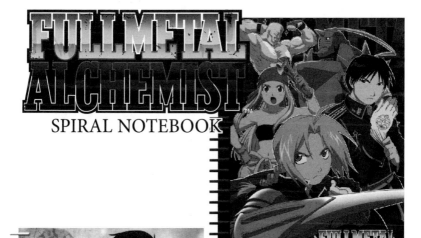

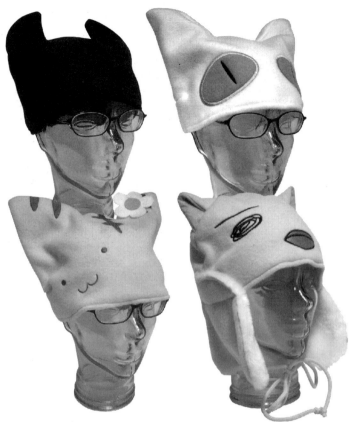

STOP!
YOU'RE READING THE WRONG WAY!

This is the end of the book! In Japan, manga is generally read from right to left. All reading starts on the upper right corner, and ends on the lower left. American comics are generally read from left to right, starting on the upper left of each page. In order to preserve the true nature of the work, we printed this book in a right to left fashion. Those who are unfamiliar with manga may find this confusing at first, but once you start getting into the story, you will wonder how you ever read manga any other way!

KA
BB

THIS QUESTIONNAIRE IS REDEEMABLE FOR:

KAMUI Volume 3 Dust Jacket

Broccoli Books Questionnaire

Fill out and return to Broccoli Books to receive your corresponding dust jacket!*

PLEASE MAIL THE COMPLETE FORM, ALONG WITH UNUSED UNITED STATES POSTAGE STAMPS WORTH $1.50 ENCLOSED IN THE ENVELOPE TO:**

Broccoli International
Attn: Broccoli Books Dust Jacket Committee
P.O. Box 66078
Los Angeles, CA 90066

(Please write legibly)

Name: ______________________________

Address: ______________________________

City, State, Zip: ______________________________

E-mail: ______________________________

Gender: ☐ Male ☐ Female **Age:** _______

(If you are under 13 years old, parental consent is required)

Parent/Guardian signature: ______________________________

Occupation: ______________________________

Where did you hear about this title?

☐ Magazine (Please specify): ______________________________

☐ Flyer from: a store convention club other: ______________________________

☐ Website (Please specify): ______________________________

☐ At a store (Please specify): ______________________________

☐ Word of Mouth

☐ Other (Please specify): ______________________________

Where was this title purchased? (If known)

____

Why did you buy this title?

____

____

CUT ALONG HERE

How would you rate the following features of this manga?

	Excellent	Good	Satisfactory	Poor
Translation	☐	☐	☐	☐
Art quality	☐	☐	☐	☐
Cover	☐	☐	☐	☐
Extra/Bonus Material	☐	☐	☐	☐

What would you like to see improved in Broccoli Books manga?

____

Would you recommend this manga to someone else? ☐ Yes ☐ No

What related products would you be interested in?

☐ Posters ☐ Apparel Other: ______________________________

Which magazines do you read on a regular basis?

____

What manga titles would you like to see in English?

____

Favorite manga titles: ______________________________

Favorite manga artists: ______________________________

What race/ethnicity do you consider yourself? (Please check one)

☐ Asian/Pacific Islander ☐ Native American/Alaskan Native

☐ Black/African American ☐ White/Caucasian

☐ Hispanic/Latino ☐ Other: ______________________________

Final comments about this manga:

____

____

____

Thank you!

* While supplies last.

** For residents of Canada, please send an International Reply Coupon (IRC) of $3.00 US made out to "Broccoli International."

All information provided will be used for internal purposes only. We will not sell or otherwise divulge any of the information.

Requests not in compliance with all terms of this form will not be acknowledged or returned. All submissions are subject to verification and become the property of Broccoli International USA. Fraudulent submission, including use of multiple addresses or P.O. boxes to obtain additional Broccoli International USA information or offers may result in prosecution. Broccoli International USA reserves the right to withdraw or modify any terms of this form. Void where prohibited, taxed, or restricted by law. Broccoli International USA will not be liable for lost, misdirected, mutilated, illegible, incomplete, or postage-due mail. Dust jacket offer is only available to residents of the United States and Canada. For updates to the rules and regulations, please see www.broccolibooks.com.

CUT ALONG HERE

KAMUI
[3]
Shingo Nanami
10
the chosen path
11
fabricated reality
12
beyond the visible
13
transfiguration
14
my wish
CONTENTS

Wi [illegible] dem dornigen Weg.